DISCOVERING CORAL REEFS

by Charis Mather

Minneapolis, Minnesota

Credits

All images are courtesy of Shutterstock.com, unless otherwise specified. With thanks to Getty Images, Thinkstock Photo, and iStockphoto. Recurring – Net Vector, Baskiabat, NotionPic, PCH.Vector, Latelier, Susann Guenther. Cover – FrentaN, Keat Eung, Severin Benz. 2–3 – stockphoto-graf. 4–5 – alexanderwhite. 6–7 – Leonardo Gonzalez, PHONT. 8–9 – Antonio Martin, Beskova Ekaterina, tubuceo. 10–11 – Kurit afshen, Photobe. 12–13 – Ethan Daniels, Miroslav Halama, Valeriia Soloveva. 14–15 – BlueOrange Studio, Subphoto.com. 16–17 – Willyam Bradberry. 18–19 – Adam Ke, Oleg Kovtun Hydrobio, Tiago Sa Brito. 20–21 – Gialdini Luca, Rich Carey. 22–23 – Nonnakrit, Sergei25.

Bearport Publishing Company Product Development Team

Publisher: Jen Jenson; Director of Product Development: Spencer Brinker; Managing Editor: Allison Juda; Editor: Cole Nelson; Associate Editor: Naomi Reich; Associate Editor: Tiana Tran; Designer: Kim Jones; Designer: Kayla Eggert; Designer: Steve Scheluchin; Production Specialist: Owen Hamlin

Library of Congress Cataloging-in-Publication Data

Names: Mather, Charis, 1999- author.
Title: Discovering coral reefs / by Charis Mather.
Description: Fusion books. | Minneapolis, Minnesota : Bearport Publishing Company, [2026] | Series: See-gulls ocean tours | Includes index.
Identifiers: LCCN 2025000999 (print) | LCCN 2025001000 (ebook) | ISBN 9798895770221 (library binding) | ISBN 9798895774533 (paperback) | ISBN 9798895771396 (ebook)
Subjects: LCSH: Coral reefs and islands--Juvenile literature. | Coral reef animals--Juvenile literature. | Deep-sea ecology--Juvenile literature. | Deep-sea animals--Juvenile literature.
Classification: LCC GB461 .M38 2026 (print) | LCC GB461 (ebook) | DDC 577.7/89--dc23/eng/20250123
LC record available at https://lccn.loc.gov/2025000999
LC ebook record available at https://lccn.loc.gov/2025001000

© 2026 BookLife Publishing
This edition is published by arrangement with BookLife Publishing.

North American adaptations © 2026 Bearport Publishing Company. All rights reserved. No part of this publication may be reproduced in whole or in part, stored in any retrieval system, or transmitted in any form or by any means, electronic, mechanical, photocopying, recording, or otherwise, without written permission from the publisher. Bearport Publishing is a division of FlutterBee Education Group.

For more information, write to Bearport Publishing, 3500 American Blvd W, Suite 150, Bloomington, MN 55431.

CONTENTS

All Aboard! 4
For Your Information . . .6
Coral Polyps 8
Sea Anemones 10
Fish 12
Manta Rays. 14
Turtles 16
Sea Stars 18
Octopuses 20
Back on Land! 22
Glossary 24
Index 24

ALL ABOARD!

Ahoy there! I am Captain Gulliver, and this is my ship. Welcome aboard! My crew and I are happy to have you join us on a See-Gulls Ocean Tour.

FOR YOUR INFORMATION

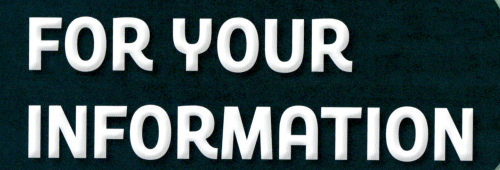

Coral reefs are often found in **shallow** coastal areas. The water there is warmer because it gets more sunlight than the deep, open ocean.

The Great Barrier Reef, off the coast of Australia, is the world's largest coral reef.

CORAL POLYPS

Although coral reefs look like colorful rocks, they are actually made up of animals called coral polyps. These animals have soft bodies and hard outer skeletons. Over time, their skeletons join together to form reefs.

SOFT BODIES

HARD SKELETON

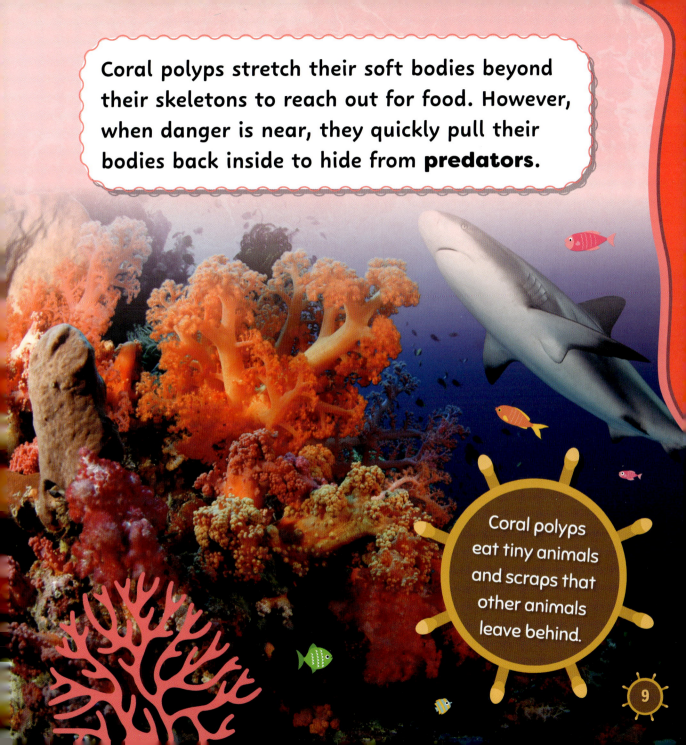

Coral polyps stretch their soft bodies beyond their skeletons to reach out for food. However, when danger is near, they quickly pull their bodies back inside to hide from **predators**.

Coral polyps eat tiny animals and scraps that other animals leave behind.

SEA ANEMONES

Corals are not the only reef creatures that do not look like animals. Sea anemones (uh-NEM-uh-neez) have many long, noodle-shaped **tentacles**.

SEA ANEMONE

There are more than 1,000 kinds of sea anemones.

Sea anemone tentacles can sting, which helps the animals keep predators away. However, clown fish can touch the tentacles. These fish don't feel the sting and live among anemones to stay safe.

CLOWN FISH WITH SEA ANEMONES

Those fish aren't clowning around!

FISH

Thousands of different kinds of fish live in coral reefs. Reef fish often have bright colors. This helps them blend in with the corals.

I was going to catch a snack, but those fish are hard to see.

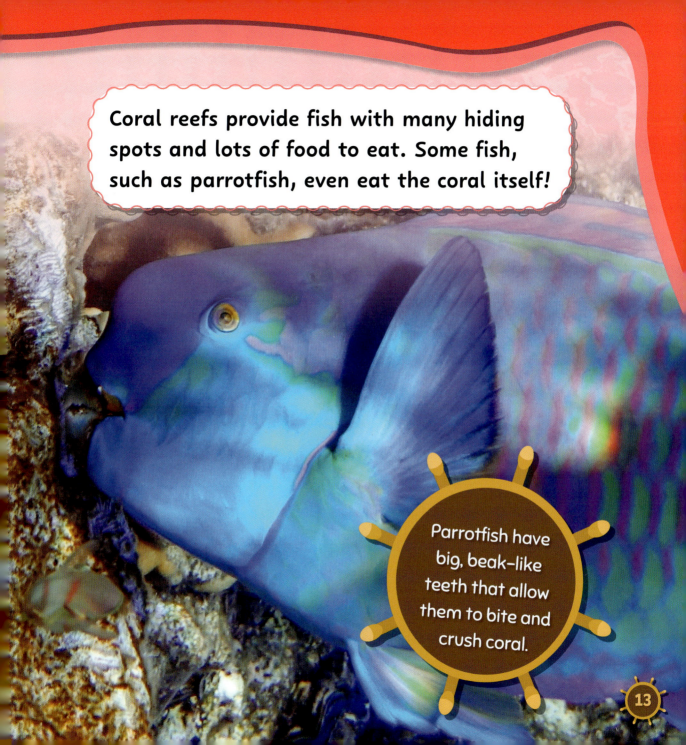

Coral reefs provide fish with many hiding spots and lots of food to eat. Some fish, such as parrotfish, even eat the coral itself!

Parrotfish have big, beak-like teeth that allow them to bite and crush coral.

MANTA RAYS

Some of the most well-known reef animals are manta rays. These large, flat fish can grow up to 18 feet (5 m) across. Despite their size, manta rays are not dangerous to humans. They eat mostly tiny ocean creatures.

That's a-ray-zing!

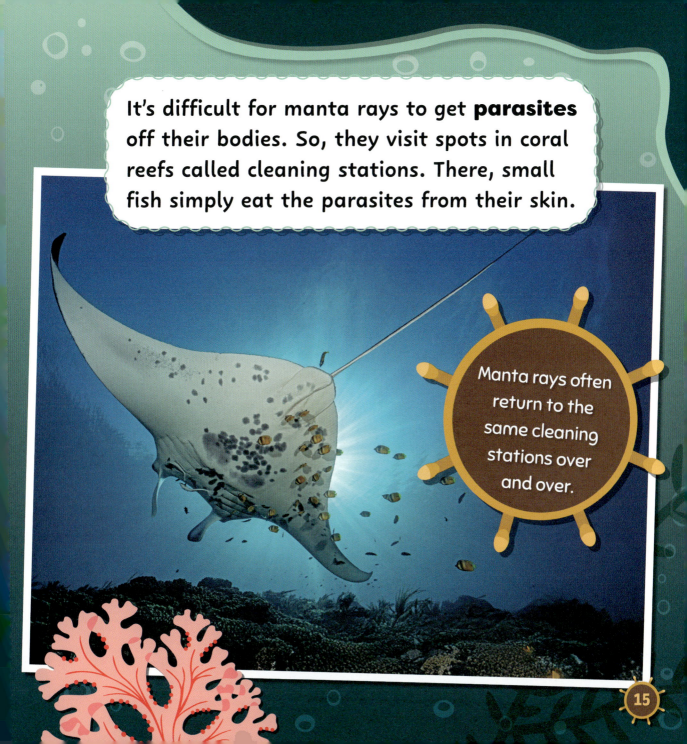

It's difficult for manta rays to get **parasites** off their bodies. So, they visit spots in coral reefs called cleaning stations. There, small fish simply eat the parasites from their skin.

Manta rays often return to the same cleaning stations over and over.

TURTLES

Sea turtles are very important to coral reefs. They eat some of the plants and animals that can quickly overgrow around a reef. This helps give the slow-growing coral polyps space in the reef.

The **nutrients** in sea turtle poop also help coral reefs stay healthy.

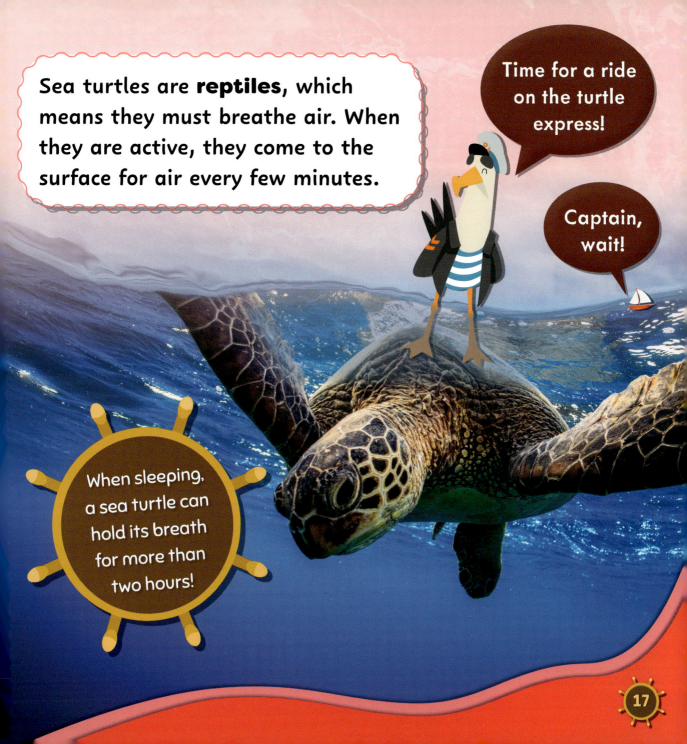

SEA STARS

That's a lot of arms!

If you look closely at the bottom of the reef, you might spot some sea stars clinging to the rocks and coral. Most sea stars have 5 arms, although some can grow as many as 40.

Sea stars have lots of **suckers** on their arms. They use them to slowly crawl around and to pry open the shells of **prey**, such as clams.

SUCKERS

If a sea star loses an arm, it can often grow it back.

OCTOPUSES

Octopuses also have many arms and can be found in coral reefs. These animals use their eight arms to crawl around and trap prey.

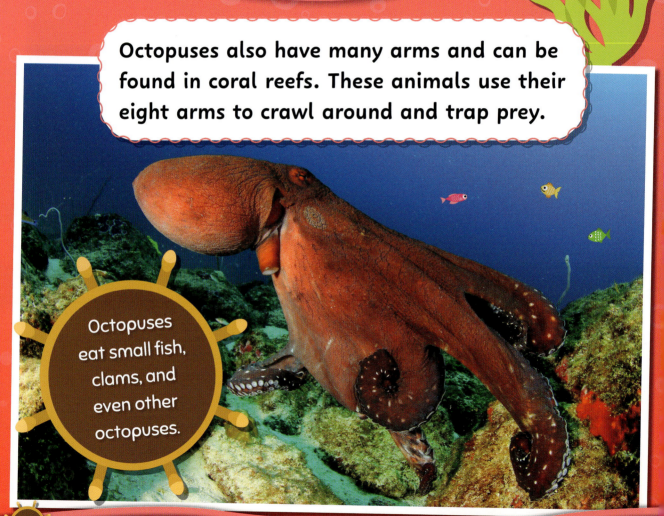

Octopuses eat small fish, clams, and even other octopuses.

Octopuses are great at hiding in plain sight. They can change the color and **texture** of their skin to blend in with rocks and corals. This helps them hide from predators, such as sharks.

BACK ON LAND!

We have reached the end of today's tour. Let's head back to land. We hope you enjoyed learning about the ocean's wonderful coral reefs!

GLOSSARY

nutrients substances that plants and animals need to grow and be healthy

parasites creatures that live on or in other living things and harm them

predators animals that hunt and eat other animals

prey animals that are hunted and eaten by other animals

reptiles cold-blooded animals that have scaly skin and use lungs to breathe

shallow not deep

suckers rounded parts of an animal's body used to grip things

tentacles long, bendy, armlike body parts of some animals

texture the feel or look of something

INDEX

arms 18–20
clown fish 11
parasites 15
parrotfish 13
predators 9, 11, 21
skeletons 8–9
sting 11
suckers 19
teeth 13
tentacles 10–11